T0354433

BEYOND RECOVERY

THE QUEST FOR SERENITY

GEORGE E. GRIFFIN, MD

BALBOA.
PRESS

A DIVISION OF HAY HOUSE

Balboa Press books may be ordered through booksellers or by contacting:

Balboa Press
A Division of Hay House
1663 Liberty Drive
Bloomington, IN 47403
www.balboapress.com
1 (877) 407-4847

Print information available on the last page.

ISBN: 978-1-5043-7344-9 (sc)
ISBN: 978-1-5043-7345-6 (hc)
ISBN: 978-1-5043-7352-4 (e)

Library of Congress Control Number: 2017901118

Balboa Press rev. date: 02/18/2017

Dedicated to

¤

Maripat Griffin Hyatt
1962-2016

¤

My Muse

TABLE OF CONTENTS

PERSPECTIVE

TOOLS

FOREWORD

Since this book is intended for those already actively involved in the 12 Step process I've chosen to write in the first person as is customary in the program. Just about everything in the book is material I've learned from my medical training, attendance at 12 Step meetings, program retreats, and addiction focused workshops and courses over the past 45 years. Some of the material is sourced from books but for the most part this offering conforms to the program recommendation to confine one's sharing to our "experience, strength and hope."

Some of what is presented may be unfamiliar territory for the reader but all of the material is part of the collective wisdom of the recovery movement. As a physician with over 45 years of active involvement in many different segments of the recovery community I've come to appreciate both their diversity as well as common purpose.

I've been to meetings and 12 Step events in many foreign countries as well as various regions of the USA. While the substance or behaviors addressed may have varied, the core principles and intent of the meetings have all been the same. In all cases, the gatherings have echoed the same truth: — That we were addicted and could not manage our lives. That no human power could relieve our disease. God could and would if God were sought. That is the core truth of all the recovery programs. What this book attempts to provide is additional insights and tools that will expand one's ability to make the greatest use of the opportunity that was offered when we all walked through the doors of our first meeting.

Those who have been released from the bondage of their compulsion for the most part are grateful for the ability to live reasonably normal lives. Unfortunately, the underlying issues that led to their addiction, and the consequences of years of active addiction, tend to confer a real lasting burden that despite committed use of traditional recovery tools, leaves the individuals with an emotional hangover of unresolved issues. Regular meeting attendance and working the steps goes a long way in resolving some of this burden but in my experience it is rare to find members that are truly at peace and have reached the higher potentials possible in the recovery process. It is for those who want more than just contented sobriety that this book is presented.

Deep within all humans is a reflection of their Creator. This expression of Divinity is hidden under layers of learned software programs accumulated from our life experiences as well as our culture. It is these ego-driven programs that interfere with our ability to fully grasp the presence of Divinity within. This is true for all humans, not just those with the disease of addiction. For most non-addicts, there is little impetus to clear away these obstructions. For the addict, it's a very different matter. Not only have addicts had to face the reality that they were unlikely to achieve sustained abstinence without the help of a "Power greater than themselves," they have also had to actively deal with the wreckage of their past if they were to have any hope of experiencing peace of mind. This book is intended to carry what those in recovery have already achieved to a higher level. There really are no limits to what can be achieved in recovery as it says on page 84 in **"The Big Book, Alcoholics Anonymous,"** "if we work for them."

PERSPECTIVE

OUTSIDE THE BOX

If nothing changes nothing changes. How many times have we heard that at meetings? I remember an old-timer telling a newcomer, "The only thing we're going to ask you to do is to change your whole life." Anyone who has been around the recovery process for any appreciable time knows the wisdom of this statement.

This book is all about making substantive life changes at many levels. Most of what will be offered will not seem dramatic or difficult, but I can assure the reader that absorbing and implementing some or all of these insights and recommendations has a high probability of creating very positive changes to the trajectory of one's life.

A key to viewing and implementing what's being

offered is the willingness to try things outside our current comfort zone. All of what's offered below are concepts and tools being utilized by numerous people in various recovery communities. Each has shown the potential to assist the individual in achieving a more balanced and serene recovery.

THE NATURE OF
ADDICTION

I'd like to clarify something that is largely overlooked or ignored by a substantial segment of the recovery community. Almost all program groups identify themselves as dealing with an addiction to a specific substance or behavior. The meetings are identified as being for an alcoholic, compulsive overeater, love and sex addict, etc. While this is very effective in helping the suffering addict find their way to the program, it tends to overlook a grander reality. The disease of addiction is bigger than any one of its physical or social manifestations. Once the disease is in place, even if the addict shows little tendency to indulge in any other form of addictive or compulsive behavior, the tendency to do so is already in place and will emerge given the opportunity.

Here is a key takeaway. The disease is addiction, not alcoholism or drug addiction or inability to eat rationally. All those addictions and many more are present to a greater or lesser degree in all who have developed addictive disease. Given the right circumstances, any one of them can creep in to replace those that may currently be in remission. True abstinence is not simply removing the compulsion to use our primary substance or behavior. It means having reached a level in the recovery process where we no longer have the need to use any mechanism to escape.

That all in recovery have the tendency to switch addictions is a hard-to-deny reality. How many have found themselves not drinking but now consuming 10 cups of coffee a day, or putting on significant weight by enjoying a pint of ice cream every evening, or ingesting an extra meal at the pancake house with the gang after the meeting? How many compulsive overeaters find it easier to stay on their food plan if they include wine as part of the plan? In my experience, such behaviors are common but not readily identified as problematic or as having switched addictions.

I remember being at an AA meeting in the spring of 1976 when a member of the group made a remarkable statement as to why we hadn't seen him for a while. Hal related that he'd started going to OA as well as AA and replied, "I'm taking my addictions in the order in which they were killing me." At the time I laughed, but over the years I've come to appreciate the deep wisdom of that statement. The many-faceted nature of addictive disease is a tender trap and few in recovery haven't taken the bait.

The purpose of all addictions, be it to a substance or a behavior, is to still unpleasant emotional chatter in the mind. Once the addictive dynamic is firmly in place, unless the addict finds healthy ways to reduce the mental noise, they will either live in a state of emotional discomfort, or will find themselves falling prey to one or more of the other addictive processes in their quest for emotional relief.

It's not necessary to understand the details of how the mind is emotionally wired to understand where the mental noise comes from. Many of us heard in school that the psyche is made up of three main operative elements—the ego that we use to manage day to day experiences, a repressed pure predatory animal element called the id, and an overall modulating element called the super ego or conscience. The ego's primary purpose is survival and over the millennia, it has learned to use pleasure and gain to achieve that goal. The ego has no concept of a Higher Power since it thinks it is totally responsible for its own survival. For the most part, the ego functions very much like a self-centered animal and is rarely content with its circumstances. Like most animals, untamed, it can be not only disruptive, but dangerous.

Bill Wilson, the co-founder of AA, was once asked if he could summarize the AA program process in a few words. His answer: "It's all about deflation of the ego at depth." What Bill was suggesting was that in order to achieve reasonable emotional sobriety the recovering addict needs to find ways of stilling the mental noise that is a dominant feature of the active ego. That is the purpose of the 12 steps and the many adjunctive recovery tools that have been added to the recovery process over the decades.

The ego, at its core, is really just an evolved animal. All animal species from bacteria to humans do not have the capacity to generate their own food. Plants can produce their own nutrients through the process of photosynthesis but animals lack that ability. Therefore, in order to survive they must search out a source of food and find ways of staying safe as they forage. Over the millennia, as animal species evolved, they learned more effective search tools and ways to protect themselves during the search. The most evolved animal species, we humans, still at our emotional core manifest those basic instincts, to find what we feel we need to survive and to stay safe in the process. The amazing complexity of the human body and mind center around these two most basic, core, instinctual drives.

Unfortunately, the evolved ego has somehow gotten its priorities distorted. Despite being surrounded by ample sources of nutrients and all the necessary elements for its survival it still thinks like a primitive animal. Over time its insatiable urge to forage has transitioned from searching for physical food to a need to find or create emotional food. The ego has actually evolved sophisticated mechanisms to create the psychic food it intuits it needs to survive. The unfortunate reality is that the main way it does this is by creating trouble. The evolved ego seeks its food in conflict, chaos, emotionality and all the other mental gyrations we all experience as part of being human. Put succinctly, the ego feeds itself by 'juicing off' the day-to-day conflicts and challenges of life. If there isn't a problem to juice off it will do what it can to create one. As one wag said at a meeting, "my ego is a problem-seeking missile." The essence of the recovery process is to tame the unruly ego until it becomes relatively silent revealing the true core of our humanity which is stillness, peace and joy.

CONCEPT OF WELLNESS

For those whose lives have been transformed by the recovery process there is little question that simply stopping the consumption of their drug has been life-changing. There is very little in one's life that an active addiction doesn't impact negatively, so simply becoming abstinent is a real game changer. But as those whose recovery has extended significantly beyond the initial euphoria over getting clean can attest, becoming abstinent is only the first rung on the ladder we must climb to achieve any reasonable quality of living. That is what the journey we call recovery is all about.

What are we talking about when we use the term recovery? Obviously, it's more than being abstinent. Is it now being able to do the things that our addictions made difficult or impossible? Of course, and more. I think the answer is best captured by The Promises on pages 83 and 84 of the **"Big Book"** of AA. "We are going to know a new freedom and a new happiness." You bet. "We will intuitively know how to handle situations which used to baffle us." Absolutely. "Are these extravagant promises?" Absolutely not. In fact, none of the promises is over-stated, as anyone who has made the recovery process the centerpiece of their lives can attest. As the **"Big Book"** states, "They are being fulfilled among us - sometimes quickly, sometimes slowly. They will always materialize if we work for them." One thing should be noted when reading The Promises. They are all open-ended statements. They are assertions that suggest that each promise can be realized at ever greater, deeper and more robust levels over time, if one continues to expand their involvement in the recovery process.

I would like to add an observation from my years of medical practice to our discussion of achieving the promises. People came to my practice because they were physically sick or emotionally troubled and were asking for help in finding relief. But over the years very few ever came asking how to structure their lives so as to not get sick, or for help in achieving the fullest measure of wellness. Unfortunately, it's been my experience that a majority of those entering recovery view success in the program in a similar way.

If we step back and recall the discussions we've been part of at most meetings over the years, it would be hard not to conclude the recovery paradigm is based primarily on how to transition from being an active addict to maintaining a life of sustained abstinence. There is no question that achieving abstinence must be the top priority, but what else does the average addict desire to achieve through the recovery process? Although at meetings some attention may be given to what is possible in recovery, it's rare to attend a meeting where substantial attention is paid to what should be the goal for all in recovery: to not only be abstinent but to be truly well in mind, body and spirit.

Let me suggest that any program member with a substantial period of sustained sobriety who doesn't have as their goal, and measure program success as experiencing a steady expansion of The Promises being fulfilled in their lives, is settling for a lot less than what the program has to offer. This book centers around the reality that we are all designed to be well, even the recovering addict. No one who reaches the doors of a 12 Step meeting needs to fail to achieve not only sustained abstinence, but also to experience a life filled with an ever expanding measure of The Promises that are the capstone of the recovery process.

PARADIGMS

A paradigm is a way of looking at things to accomplish something. For example, in the early days of building automobiles the paradigm was to build them one at a time, piece by piece. Then along came Henry Ford who introduced the idea of making them on an assembly line with different people adding specific parts. The assembly line represented a significant paradigm change.

We are surrounded by paradigms such as the familiar patterns of how we communicate, bank, get health care, travel, etc. But think back as far as you can. Are we doing things the same way now as when we were younger? As someone over 80 I can say a resounding, "Heck, no." A great example of an ever-expanding paradigm has been the rapid increase in the ways in which we can communicate. So paradigm changes are occurring all the time.

Do you know someone who doesn't have or refuses to use a cell phone and will only use a land line? One could say they have paradigm allegiance to the old way of doing things. Do you know someone who isn't willing to even look at the newer communication tools and advances available? You might say they have a case of paradigm blindness. The important point here is that we live in a world of expanding paradigms ranging from styles of communication to how kids are taught math in school. We have people who welcome paradigm change and quickly adapt to the new ways and we have people who vigorously resist, and maintain allegiance to the old ways. We also have people who for whatever reason just don't pay attention to what's unfolding as things change all around them.

Why do paradigms change? The obvious intention of any change is to make things better, faster, more efficient, more effective, or to solve a problem. We like to call these changes making progress. But do all newly introduced ways of doing things result is positive change? Think about that question for a while. How many programs introduced by the government just move things around and often actually create unintended consequences that may be more problematic than the original issue? A lot, if not, most. So there are paradigm shifts that really don't move things forward or improve things at all.

Here is a key insight. Paradigm shifts, to be effective, all require new, expanded ways of viewing the problem to be solved. Trying to solve a problem from the same old way of looking at things will only produce similar results. If nothing changes, nothing changes may sound like a silly statement, but unfortunately, we live in a world where paradigm allegiance and paradigm blindness are common. A majority of humanity spends their lifetime searching for solutions to life's conundrums while still using the same tools that created the problems in the first place. No problem can be solved from the paradigm that created it. Solving problems requires finding more effective tools and adopting newer, more expansive ways of thinking.

The recovery paradigm has changed significantly since Bill and Bob met. The history of the program suggests that we have been graced with ever-expanding insights, not only in how to help the sick and suffering addict find abstinence, but also in how those in recovery might achieve a more serene way of living. We need to ask ourselves, 'Have I been guilty of paradigm blindness in ignoring these evolutionary changes? Have I been guilty of paradigm allegiance to the limiting paradigm that suggests that contented sobriety is all that is really possible in recovery? Am I committed to constantly searching for more effective tools to augment my recovery?"

CONTENT VS CONTEXT

A good way of becoming comfortable with embracing positive paradigm shifts is through an understanding of the difference between the concepts of content and context. Let's go back to pre- and post-Henry Ford's introduction of the assembly line. From the time of their invention, making cars at a profit was the desired goal. The intention to make a car was the context or goal, and putting its parts together the content, or processes necessary to achieving the goal. In the early days, people could make them one at a time and make a profit. Along came Henry Ford who had an expansive idea. He reasoned if he could streamline the building process and make it more efficient, he could make more cars for less money and make a greater profit. Under his way of thinking the context was now efficiently making a lot of cars using the new paradigm of assembly line production and the content was now a steady flow of cars. Sure, the cars still have individual parts but there has been a significant shift in the context of how cars were produced. In this example, it is clear that as the paradigm shifted, the big picture or context expanded.

This simple concept of creating a more efficient and productive context for managing the content of life is the eight lane super highway to a progressively more expansive way of being. Our lives should be filled with a zest for finding and introducing a progression of ever expanding and effective paradigms of living. Knowledge alone won't keep us abstinent but having an ever- increasing grasp of the big picture, available through the recovery process, sure helps one find better ways of achieving that goal.

THE JOURNEY

Each human represents an expression of both evolutionary history as well as a personal life story. Down through the ages in all cultures, humans have asked themselves the same questions. Why are we here? Where did we come from? Where do we go when the body dies? The consensus arrived at by the greatest thinkers over time is that we are here to learn. They suggested that the things we experience in life are simply presenting us with events that contain lessons to be learned.

Evolution is, after all, the history of various species who, through trial and error, learned better and more effective ways of living and thus prospered. Those species that did not learn or adjust eventually disappeared. In many ways our individual lives represent and follow the same script. Just as humanity evolved as it learned various essential lessons, so too, do individuals prosper as they gain an expanded perspective and learn how to use more effective tools.

One way of visualizing both the evolutionary history of our species as well as that of each individual is to view the evolutionary process as being metaphorically similar to climbing one of the great mountains of the world. The pictures we see of a majestic mountain are often from a distance. When shown a close-up view, it's usually the windy, snow-swept peak of the mountain way above the tree line. But these pictures really hide the true expanse and various regions of these giants.

The roads leading up to these great mountains usually go through deep jungles and swamps created by the heavy run off of water from the mountain. As a climber gets to the base of the mountain they are exposed to adverse temperatures and conditions far different than they will experience at the upper reaches of the mountain. As they start their climb they move though deep forests which, like the jungles below, make it virtually impossible for them to have any real appreciation for the world outside the mountain. As they reach higher elevations the trees start to get smaller and to thin out a bit, offering the climber their first glimpse of the world beyond the confines of the mountain. Still higher up, the trees start to give way to bushes, and now the expanse of the surrounding vista becomes more visible. Once the climber reaches the tree line, there are few obstructions to their being able to grasp the big picture view of not only where they are in relation to the world, but of the territory yet to be traversed on their way to the summit.

This metaphor of climbing a great mountain offers both a big picture perspective of human evolution over the millennia as well as the personal journey each human makes in their lifetime. It allows us to put into context the evolution of the human species over the eons, as well as the personal journey we all must take if we are ever to reach the pristine reaches above the tree line. It is also the story of the recovery process.

As our species has evolved over the eons, the majority of its history has been spent deep in the swamps and jungles at the base of the mountain. Even going back three millennia, the vast majority of mankind still had not yet reached the level of the deep forest. It was not until roughly 1500 years ago that a significant number of our species even got to enter the forested area. I would like to say that mankind has climbed its way past the swamps and forest but unfortunately, that's not the case.

What is fortunate for our species is that for at least the last 10,000 years, there have been unique individuals who have traversed to above the tree line and even rarer still, a few have even reached the summit of the mountain. These Avatars such as Lord Buddha, Lord Krishna and the Lord Jesus Christ have told us with great clarity the Truths they understood from their perspective at the summit. They have not only passed down these essential Truths but have shown us by example what is possible for us humans. They all taught that it is possible for each of us to reach the summit.

THE PURGATORIAL MIX
THAT IS HUMANITY

Let's look again at the mountain metaphor, but this time in a single stop-frame. This grand spectrum that represents the various levels of human evolution is in fact a realistic way of describing the current evolutionary distribution of the world's population. There are a great many population centers that exist at the lowest levels of the mountain, as well as a lesser number high enough to be able to get a glimpse of the world beyond the mountain. There are even a rare few groups of humans who are at or near the very top. Unfortunately, the vast majority of humanity is still functioning at the level of the swamps and woods where it's not possible to gain a realistic perspective about the greater world beyond the mountain. One might say, they can't see the forest—the big picture—because of the trees. I can assert with reasonable assurance that anyone with sufficient self-interest to be reading this book has climbed out of the deep woods and has the potential to evolve emotionally and spiritually to the tree line and should settle for achieving nothing less during this lifetime.

This way of looking at the world's populations does not say those at lower levels in their emotional and spiritual evolution are lesser than those further up the mountain. It just recognizes that we humans are all here to work through various lessons as we traverse the mountain, and some have just progressed further than others in the growth process. Every human, no matter what level they've reached, has work to do at that level in order to make the ascent to the next rung up the evolutionary ladder.

Let's carry this metaphor just a bit further. We have suggested that the people at the lowest levels are surrounded by deep jungles and swamps, so their ability to achieve any perspective is extremely limited. Contrast them to those higher up where the vegetation has thinned out and they can grasp what's unfolding in a more realistic way. Each would likely say that what they were experiencing was what the real world is like, despite the fact that each is experiencing the world quite differently.

This is a key insight. As we climb the mountain of the evolutionary process, we think that what we perceive is the only reality. From our narrow and limited perspective, we can easily have trouble understanding that someone at a different level, or a higher elevation, might experience things quite differently. This is a prime factor in the human propensity to become intolerant: a kind of paradigm allegiance or blindness if you like. The best solution to this narrow way of thinking is to move further up the mountain so that we may see and understand the world in a progressively more realistic way. It follows then that the problems of each paradigm are best solved by moving to a higher paradigm. Issues that can't be solved at one level become more obvious and resolvable at a higher level.

This way of viewing the world as being composed of a ladder of ascending paradigms helps us understand the political, economic and social chaos that fills the daily news cycle. The world we live in is a true purgatorial mix of peoples whose progress in the evolutionary process is widely divergent. What will work to solve problems at one level might not work at another. How one at a given paradigm envisions a solution to an issue, for another paradigm, may in fact make things worse. This awareness suggests we all step back and become less judgmental about the struggles our society and various cultures face in trying to find solutions to major issues.

LINEAR VS NON-LINEAR

We live in a world that bathes us with information, colors, sounds and the faces of friends. This is a world we can record, measure and understand down to the sub molecular level. However, we humans also experience life at another level, a level we can't see or measure. We experience Love, Kindness, Compassion, Forgiveness, and other things that really matter but can't be measured or dissected.

The first of these two categories is what is called the linear world. It's the world of things we can see, taste, touch and measure. The second paradigm is the non-linear realm, a realm of qualities we know about, because they are part of us, but we can't see with our eyes or measure with an instrument.

These are the linear and non-linear paradigms of our world. What follows is a critical distinction between the two paradigms. The only way to truly know something is to be it. For example, you can study cats all your life and get a PhD in cat physiology, you can know everything there is to know about cats, but the only way to truly understand cat-ness is to be a cat. You can understand a lot about cats and you can measure a cat's physiology and anatomy down to the molecular level, but the only way to truly understand what it's like to be a cat is to be a cat. The bottom line is cats are measurable but not truly knowable. This principle applies to everything in the linear world. Things in the linear world are measurable but their true essence is not knowable. What we see and smell and taste are things we can measure but cannot know. As odd as it may seem this is a true statement.

So what about the non-linear dimension? Love is something we can experience but can't measure. Sure, we can see the daily quote in the paper, "Love is———," but as a popular song says, "I want to know what Love is; I want you to show me." It sure isn't measurable in any objective way but we can know it through experiencing it and showing it to others. We can truly know it because it's what we are. The same is true of all the rest of the qualities of the non-linear realm; they can be known because we can experience and be them but they are not measurable.

Why is the above distinction between the linear

and non-linear domains important? If you're a carpenter, the linear is exceedingly important. To know how to measure a board, read plans and pull all the elements together is essential in building a house. But what if you're someone in recovery whose life has been drastically limited by what led up to, as well as the consequences of your disease? It's the things of the non-linear world that they have most missed out on, and that the addict understands the least because of that lack of experience. It's also the primary area to be explored in recovery if one wishes to get past just being abstinent.

Recovery to a level of serene wellness is a recovery of the spirit as well as the body and mind. It's the non-linear qualities of Love, Kindness, Compassion, Impartiality and Forgiveness that move our recovery from functional contentment to a level of serene peacefulness. Understanding and manifesting these qualities is the essence of true wellness. New Age thinking suggests that wellness has mostly to do with diet, exercise and lifestyle, all linear concepts. I would argue that true wellness is freedom of the spirit and that can only be achieved by embracing the non-linear realms.

One can experience poverty, live with a disability, be aware one has a terminal disease, and yet if one has a good grasp of the non-linear qualities of what we are at our core, then one can be at peace with what is occurring in the linear domain.

PERCEPTION AND POSITIONALITY

We have discussed in a previous section that we humans see things through our own individual perceptual lens and that lens depends on where we are in our climb up the mountain of consciousness. What one perceives and experiences as reality at one level of the mountain will not be the same should we climb to a higher level or for that matter descend back to a lower level.

This principle also applies to how the human ego presents, and the challenges we face in defusing its disruptive impact on our recovery. Although the ego will always have as its central focus, survival, pleasure and gain, how these manifest at the lowest levels of the mountain will be very different from how these manifest up close to the tree line. The options available to the ego to juice for emotional food change as we move up through each level. While at its very core, everyone's ego is about the same, the expression of the ego varies greatly depending on how emotionally and spiritually evolved we are in our ascent up the mountain.

As Bill Wilson suggested, we need to defuse the ego's animal-like behaviors by evolving to higher levels of consciousness where it can be exposed to a more expansive reality. As long as we have an operative ego, we will, to some extent, be subject to its animalistic proclivities. How intrusive the ego is in our lives will depend heavily on to what extent the ego has been tamed by its exposure to reality and the resolution of its stored negative energies.

Positionality is a term that is used to describe how we humans perceive our relationship with the things around us. The ego sees anything outside what it experiences as "self" as being "other." If we remember that at its core the ego is animalistic, we can understand its primary focus will be survival and all outside itself will be constantly scrutinized to determine if it will help or hinder that survival. Over the eons of evolution, this simple animal survival mechanism has given rise to the ego experiencing itself as separate. As usual, the ego's self-centered perspective has distorted what is wholeness, into parts, in support of its survival instincts.

The grander reality is that the universe is not made up of this and that, or mine and yours, or in and out. The universe just is what it is: one grand "IS." But not to the ego. Isn't that what your mind is telling you right now as you read this? The ego's entire focus is on its self as separate from its surroundings. Experience has shown that it is this narcissistic core of the ego that gives rise to almost all of human suffering. The world that the ego perceives as separate is a world of danger and a world where it sees itself as the sole arbiter of its survival. It's a world where it needs to be right and to win at all costs. The ego has no concept of the non-linear and spirituality since it sees itself as God. The ego has little capacity to grasp the big picture that is reality because it's enclosed itself in a little self-created, self-centered box.

As we ponder these ideas we can get a deeper and more insightful understanding of just how important it is to tame the ego. In fairness, it's appropriate to be grateful for the ego's work in helping our species survive over the eons of evolution. We are asserting, however, that in large measure the human ego has outlived its usefulness. Those who have been Graced with having moved beyond the limitations of the ego, the Saints, Sages and the Mystics, have demonstrated that it's possible to function as a joyous and free human after the ego has been transcended.

Unfortunately, since the ego, at its core, is an animal, it will do everything in its power to survive and stay in control. As our ability to better perceive reality increases and we start to better and more fully understand the oneness of things, the ego will slowly lose its grip on our lives. We don't need to fight the ego; we just need to replace it with a grander perspective of reality. We need to surrender the ego's narcissistic belief that it's separate and the author of its own survival, and deepen our trust in the Loving Mercy of a Power greater the ourselves that is the true author of all things.

THE TENSION OF
THE OPPOSITES

We have discussed that it's only an ego-illusion that sees the world as made up of separate parts. In reality there are no parts, only wholeness, oneness. Yet because we are human and still have an operative ego in play, we all still experience what is wholeness, as parts and polarities. We see happy and sad, up and down, and good and bad. But if we believe the teachings of the world's Wisdom Traditions these perceptions and positionalities are illusions and to buy into them is a vanity of the ego.

How are we to deal with this conundrum? We are human, and as long as we have an ego in play, we must deal with opposites and polarities and separates. The answer is simple. We become aware that what we experience and our ego tells us is real, is in reality a house of mirrors and can be surrendered as an illusion. But you say, "How then does one function?" The answer is, we strive to position ourselves in the high ground between the opposites. Avoiding having opinions or making judgments makes it a lot easier to just be with what is; "it is what it is."

Instead of buying into good or bad, we strive to see things just as they are without judgment. The same for happy vs sad and all the other dualities. Things just are what they are. There are no dualities other than those created by the ego as part of it survival strategies. Things just are what they are.

You might ask, "What about hot vs cold?" The answer is simply that, while the concept of hot and cold is pragmatically useful on a daily basis, in reality, there is no hot or cold. There is just the relative presence or progressive absence of heat. There is only one variable, heat, not two. There is only the relative activity of the molecules. The ego's perception function uses created language to label something hot or cold based on what it thinks will provide it comfort and safety, but there is only the is-ness of temperature.

These distinctions are not just word games. They are of critical importance to our quest to free ourselves from the dominance of the ego. They are at the root of one of the most vital tools for those in recovery: acceptance. The ego is always functioning in problem-seeking mode when, in the present moment, the Now, there is only is-ness. In the Now there can be no problem or need for a label because things just are what they are. No ego spin is required.

You might come back and ask, "Well, how about win vs lose?" Here again, it's all in the eyes of the beholder. Win and lose are just words. For us at Thanksgiving dinner, enjoying a turkey is a win, but I think the turkey would suggest otherwise.

Stephen Covey, in his book, "**The Seven Habits of Highly Effective People**," really makes this point well. His fourth habit is to "Think Win-Win." Most addicts grew up in a shame-based world where the big people made the rules, always got to be right, and to win all arguments. As we humans grow, we are likely to follow a path to ensure that we get to be the one who makes the rules, be right and to win. The outcome of this very almost universal human dynamic is that life becomes viewed as a world where you are either the winner or the loser, and it's important to be the one who is right and wins. This view of life is at the root of much of human suffering.

Covey suggests that in most human exchanges, even though people perceive things quite differently there usually can be found a middle ground where both can come away feeling validated and a winner. In the situation where no middle ground could be reached there is a corollary option available: "Win-Win, No Play." We don't have to make someone wrong; we can just decide to walk away. This habit regularly practiced can be life-changing.

ACCEPTANCE

All of the 12 Step programs place a high priority on adopting a stance of acceptance of things as they are and surrendering our human feelings about what is to a higher Power. Our problems don't stem from what is. Our problems stem from our ego's reaction to what is. There is little chance of finding any level of contented sobriety without learning to live life on life's terms. Obviously acceptance is the key.

The concept of acceptance means different things to the recovering addict as their sobriety evolves. In the early years it usually means realizing the chaos they have been experiencing has been caused by their addiction. As they come alive, they start to accept that only abstinence and following a program of emotional and spiritual growth will allow them to climb out of that chaos. As their sobriety matures, they become comfortable with living in a world where many things aren't to their liking, but with acceptance, this does not upset their emotional balance or present a risk to their sobriety.

With mature sobriety, a more expanded paradigm of acceptance presents itself. One starts to understand that when one doesn't like something it has nothing to do with the reality of what that thing is, but rather, that it isn't what our ego wanted it to be. This understanding is a core principle of Buddhism, namely, "There are only two things that exist: what is and my reaction to what is." We usually can't change what is, but we can change our reaction to what is.

When we no longer have the urge to put a label or spin on what we are experiencing, we have crossed an important threshold. Whereas most humans find themselves needing to be on constant alert as they surrender life's ups and downs, with true acceptance we are now able to take a step back and just watch the experiences of life as they unfold. Being able to stay as the accepting watcher rather than the overwhelmed experiencer is the very essence of true acceptance.

LOVE

No subject has more garbage written about it than Love. This is primarily because there is a general confusion about what is meant when the word Love is used. This stems from the fact that our society has only one term for a concept that can't easily be reduced to a single word. There are other societies that have multiple words for Love that allow for more textured ways of describing its various presentations.

Our society's disconnect primarily stems from confusing love, which is principally a linear biologic instinct to mate and reproduce, with Love, which is of the non-linear realm and the very essence of Divinity. In the absence of different words these two very different presentations are written as love and Love respectively.

Human love is about nature needing us to find mates and reproduce in order to perpetuate the species. Over time, humans have morphed this simple biologic need into what is now understood as romantic love with all its rituals and emotional dynamics. It's about attachments and getting our perceived needs met. The ability to experience this aspect of our humanity is a wondrous gift as long as it's handled responsibly. Very few who find their way to a 12 Step program can honestly say they are not carrying some real baggage in relation to how they have managed these instincts. The ego has a field day juicing on the guilt and shame we generate over how we have handled ourselves in this area. For anyone looking to decrease the ego's sway in their recovery there are very few areas that will offer a better return on effort than cleaning up the wreckage from our misuse of these biologic instincts.

Maybe the most important thing that can be said about the non-linear quality we call Love is that it's the ultimate law of the Universe. Most program people who have become comfortable with the concept of a Higher Power will easily interchange the non-linear word Love for Higher Power or God. Those who have come to believe they have been relieved of the bondage of an active addiction through the Lovingness of their Higher

Power have grasped the real essence of the word Love.

True Lovingness is the very essence of the 12 Step process. It's the energy that results in the recovery miracle at 12 step meetings. This power is present no matter who is at the meeting, the language spoken or the words that are said. There is no other power strong enough to break though the stranglehold of the addictive process. That emotionally broken humans can gather together to help each other and somehow find a day of recovery is a manifestation of unconditional Lovingness. It is an aspect of Divinity that is doing for us what we can't do for ourselves.

TRUTH

We live in an age where relativism has become the norm. There was a time when a law was a law and it was to be obeyed. Now, many citizens only obey the laws that they like. They think that what their mind tells them is right or wrong is what is right for them. This way of thinking has been given the grand title of Secular Humanism. As a cartoon character might put it as he thumbed his nose at society: "You ain't the boss of me." In short, it's OK to just do your thing. Sure sounds like an out of control, narcissistic ego, doesn't it?

Obviously, in a world of over 7 billion people compartmentalized into diverse societies, there is room for a wide variation in how the world is viewed and differing cultural standards. As was pointed out in a previous section, where one stands in climbing the mountain of emotional and spiritual evolution profoundly effects the lens through which one then views the world. Is what each different person on the mountain sees as truth the same? Hardly. So does that mean there is no such thing as objective Truth? Despite what the Secular Humanists would like us to believe, the answer is a resounding "no." The challenge is not, is there objective Truth, but how are we humans with our separate lens views of the world to know what is the Truth? There are vast libraries filled with books devoted to this subject. Suffice it to say, the fully evolved Sages and Mystics of all cultures throughout recorded history have all agreed that there is an objective Truth, and it stands out as obvious when the obstruction of the human ego has been wiped aside.

What does the expanding influence of Secular Humanistic thinking mean for those in recovery in their search for true wellness? It means that in order to experience continuous growth in recovery, one must avoid the trap of Secular Humanistic thinking and become a student of Truth. It means surrendering the everyday world's arbitrary ways. Narcissistic thinking can no longer be part of our lives. It means that we need to develop a more mature sense of right and wrong and to the best of our ability obey the rules of society. It means we need to understand the essence of what the wise ones of all cultures down through the ages have taught about Spiritual Values and make them the centerpiece of our lives.

THE QUEST

We all understand the core goal of all the 12 Step Programs is abstinence from the substance or behavior that rendered our lives unmanageable. Without abstinence, very little progress can be made in restoring an individual to a reasonable level of sanity. Close behind the need for abstinence is the imperative to change many of the ways we think and manage our lives. The recovering addict needs to do what it takes to clean up the emotional, physical and social wreckage created during years of active addiction.

The Loving support of 12 Step meetings, a good sponsor and working the 12 steps most often results in continued physical and emotional sobriety and the emergence of a more rational way of living. As The Promises in the "**Big Book**" suggest, "We will know a new freedom and a new happiness." Unfortunately, although our active addiction may be in remission, the wreckage of our past is likely to still be part of the equation. Are meetings, a good sponsor and working the 12 steps sufficient to result in full recovery from the causes of our addictions and the wreckage of the past? Let's look at the record:

I've been deeply involved in the 12 Step process for over 45 years. Regular meetings, AWOL groups, retreats like the Matt Talbot Recovery Movement, as well as step study retreats have been a consistent part of my weeks. I've watched people come and go, as well as come and stay in the recovery process. Like all of us who regularly attend meetings, I've seen the miracle of abstinence manifest and people return to a more manageable way of living. Unfortunately, what I haven't seen very often is people who are no longer carrying the emotional and social consequences of their past. What I do hear is gratitude for being relieved of the bondage of active addiction, but what I don't see are people who can comfortably and honestly say they are at peace and their lives are joyful. What I've been observing for decades is people who are no longer sick, but rarely people who are really well.

The remainder of this book will try to present some of tools that are currently available that can help us reduce the bondage of the ego in order to achieve true wellness. Those I've met over the years who have made a more robust recovery and no longer carry the wounds of their past have all used some or all of these tools to achieve a full and more serene emotional, as well as physical, sobriety. The quality of their lives has improved, often dramatically.

TOOLS

IN A BOAT WITHOUT
A PADDLE

When people first show up at a 12 step program they are encouraged to just sit, relax and listen. Usually the warmth of the welcome and the positive energy they experience from the members is enough to give them hope and start them on the path. We all know that this is just the initial step, and if one has any hope of meaningful recovery, there is much that must be done to achieve what the programs offer. Recovery is a journey, not an event.

I'd like to offer another metaphor that, in my experience, provides a meaningful framework from which to view the recovery journey. It is a core teaching in all the 12 Step programs that, "We are responsible for the effort but not for the results," and another, "God is doing for us what we cannot do for ourselves." As I heard an old timer say at a meeting many years ago, "I was up the creek without a paddle and if Divinity didn't provide a push, I'd still be headed nowhere."

The old timer was right. Our recovery is like being in a boat in a river. We have no oars, paddle or engine. All we have is a rudder. The only energy that will move the boat is the current of the river. How effectively we use the boat's rudder to position ourselves in the current has a lot to do with how well and how safely we will proceed down the river. Should we choose, we can just allow the boat to drift where it might, continue downstream, or perhaps just head to the shore, or even onto the rocks. There may be rapids and white water as we journey downstream so that how well we navigate with the rudder will be critical to our safety. If the boat is overloaded, it may not handle well and at worst, may capsize. Having the essentials with us will help us survive the journey. When all is said and done, however, without the current to move us, we're going nowhere.

It is the conventional wisdom of all the 12 Step programs that the assistance of a Higher Power is essential to the recovery process. In our metaphor, a Higher Power is the current in the river. In the boat, we can choose to ignore the presence of the current, but that overlooks its importance to how our journey unfolds. Equally, just allowing ourselves to drift rudderless may even carry us into danger. On the other hand, those who work hard to position themselves effectively where the current is strongest and who have a boatload of effective tools at their disposal will likely find their journey to be uneventful and rewarding. There is an old saying that applies very well to the recovery process: "The person with the best tools usually gets the best results." Having traveled to some very primitive places, I know that great skill with primitive tools can create stunning results, but on average, I think the statement is valid and especially in recovery.

In the last few decades, recovery from addiction has been sufficiently portrayed by high profile public figures, as well as in movies and TV shows, with the result that the cultural barriers to people coming for help have been greatly reduced. In addition to cultural de-stigmatization, the last decade has seen the blossoming of a wide spectrum of additional modalities to support the recovery process. That sure wasn't so for the early decades of our various programs. Anyone who has read Bill Wilson's story knows he struggled with deep depression in addition to his alcoholism. Back then, there was little hope for someone like Bill. Fortunately for him, with the help of Fr. Bill Dowling, SJ and Dr. Harry Tiebout, MD, he was able to sufficiently recover from his depression to lead the 12 Step movement through its early years. That quality of help and so much more is now readily available to almost anyone in recovery.

One might ask the question, 'OK, if we now have knowledgeable medical help, almost universal availability of 12 Step meetings and an expanding bag of great recovery tools, why are many in recovery struggling to find peace of mind? Why is the relapse rate still so high? Why do so many who have been freed from the compulsion of one aspect of the addictive process fallen prey to another? Why do so many members of the recovery community feel the need to be on medication? Why is just reaching a life of contented abstinence considered sufficient, when the potential for a life of real serenity where one is truly happy, joyous and free is achievable?'

I think the answer to all these questions is both simple and profoundly challenging. The simple answer is that very few people in recovery realize just how much is possible in their recovery. Few fully appreciate that there is far greater joy and freedom possible for those who avail themselves of more than just doing enough to stay abstinent. My experience from thousands of program interactions over the past 45 years suggests that a high percentage of members are content with just being not sick, rather than truly well. For many, the idea that serene recovery was a possibility for someone who had experienced bankruptcy of mind, body and spirit seemed a road too far. Yet, it's our birthright as humans, and a possibility for all who find their way into the halls.

The recovery process is constantly evolving and both the tools and the potential for higher and more serene levels of recovery are evolving as well. The "road to happy destiny," the "**Big Book**" posits, is now paved with new effective tools that can better achieve the goal that Bill Wilson laid out when he said the recovery process was all about "deflation of the ego at depth." The evolution of the recovery process has entered an era where it is now possible for all in recovery to become truly happy, joyous, and free.

MEETINGS

Over the years, when my professional peers who knew I was involved with 12 Step programs would ask me, "How do those programs work?" I used to answer, with a smile, "Just fine." It wasn't till recent years when I was introduced to a theoretical physics field called Non-Linear Dynamics as well as the writings of the American Mystic, Dr. David Hawkins, that I had a clear and meaningful answer.

Non-linear Dynamics is the study of what are called "Attractor Fields." A simple way of looking at what they posit is to view the universe as made up of one large energy field, something similar to a magnetic field within which are sub-fields all the way down to the smallest aspect of our world. These "attractor fields" underlie all aspects of how the world unfolds. For example, the reason why a school of fish all swims in sync with each other, or migratory birds know when and where to relocate with the change of season, is that they are following the dictates of attractor fields.

Dr. Hawkins, whose books are described and recommended later, has written extensively about consciousness and attractor fields. One of his most important contributions is to show that the attractor field energy of consciousness ranges in power from the lowest level possible up to the infinite, and he has developed a Map of Consciousness that relates to where things fall on that scale and a way of measuring their place on the scale. Reading his book, "**Power vs Force**," spells all this out in understandable terms and offers a context that helps us better understand our experience of the world. It will also make the metaphor of the purgatorial mix of humanity climbing the mountain much more understandable.

In the matter of the 12 Step process, the level of consciousness of meetings is the level of unconditional Love. Even though the individuals who attend the meeting may be much lower on the scale, when they gather together to help each other to achieve sobriety, the attractor field of an unconditionally Loving process is present. Dr. Hawkins' work also suggests that the power of the addictive process is very strong and the only thing available of sufficient power to overcome addiction is the power of unconditional Love. It follows that as long as the addict stays close to that aspect of the 12 step process, the potential for continuous abstinence is possible. Should the addict leave the sphere of Lovingness intrinsic to meetings, the risk of relapse is high.

I've attended meetings in parts of the world where I didn't speak the language, and yet been struck by how good I felt at the end of the meeting even though, I hadn't understood a word said. That finally made sense when I learned meetings were effective primarily because they manifested unconditional Lovingness. It then became obvious that it wasn't necessary to understand a word of what was said at a meeting as long as one was present at the meeting. It was the attractor field of unconditional Lovingness within the meeting process itself that resulted in the powerful emotional lift I've always gotten from attending a meeting. I'm sure there is value in absorbing the collective wisdom that's shared at meetings, but I believe that the miracle that occurs is because those in attendance are bathed in the unconditional Lovingness of the process we call a meeting.

We currently are in an era where one can

travel to almost any part of the world and find a 12 Step gathering. Social media now offers on-line meetings and one can go to xa.com on the web and find hundreds of recorded presentations about recovery from the exceedingly diverse recovery community. We have reached a time where there is a meeting type, place and time to match anyone's unique requirements. There really are few valid reasons not to be able to get to lots of meetings.

LITERATURE

Each of the 12 Step programs have a wonderful array of insightful literature which should be read and absorbed by those seeking to expand their recovery. This wasn't so in the early years. Bill Wilson, Dr. Bob and those lucky few who found their way into the rooms depended heavily on outside literature. Over the ensuing years, the core insights of each program have been made available as program approved literature. While program literature has grown to what now represents a dependable body of work that reflects the evolved collective wisdom of our programs, just like in the early days, there is still a place for quality, recovery focused 'outside' literature as well.

Along with the advent of formal addiction treatment models and agencies, there has been a rapidly expanding body of non-program material available in books, recordings, and for free on the web. Additionally, in recent years, our society has become more open to exploring the literature and practices of the world's great Wisdom Traditions. The amount of high quality, insightful, written and recorded material available has truly reached prodigious proportions.

It has been my experience that most members of the various recovery communities tend to stick to their specific programs, **"Big Book," "12 and 12,"** and maybe a daily meditation book or two. There was a time when most programs advised their members to primarily use program literature and discouraged the introduction of non-conference approved literature at meetings. I do think this bias against outside literature has subsided a lot but still persists. An additional reason that some non-conference literature hasn't become more main stream is the general lack of familiarity with just how useful some of this material would be for all those in recovery.

What I'm suggesting is that if one wants the highest quality of sobriety and to experience The Promises as fully as possible, conference approved literature should be just the basic literature used. Obviously, once one has settled into the recovery process and gained a little momentum, becoming familiar with our specific programs literature should take priority. **"Big Book"** study groups, step meetings and newer variations like AWOL groups really are effective in deepening our understanding of the journey and clearing away some of the wreckage of our past. Clearly, our collective experience has been that use of these tools will help us transition from being a sick and suffering addict to a non-sick person with good abstinence and contented sobriety. My contention is that to reach the more serene levels of recovery, we need to go beyond what has become the mainstream norms currently in vogue in most recovery programs. We need to avail ourselves of the useful non-conference approved literature now available.

PRAYER AND MEDITATION

The first 10 steps of the program do a good job in helping us become abstinent and experience contented sobriety. Unfortunately, these psychologically structured concrete action steps are, at best, marginally successful in quieting the human ego, whose unrelenting noise has, in large measure, been at the root of our addictions. Their limited effectiveness in stilling the noise in our mind is a good example of the principle that no problem can be solved from within the same paradigm that created the problem in the first place.

It's been my experience that there are very few populations in society that have busier minds than people in recovery. If the purpose of adopting an addiction in the first place was to still the noise in our heads, what happens when we stop the addiction, sedative or behavior? The noise is back and likely much greater because of the consequences of our years of active addiction. One has only to chat with any members to realize they may be abstinent but their heads are very busy and they are really not at peace.

Active meeting attendance and working the steps has been our time honored way of moving from being in a state of constant turmoil emotionally to a place of contentment. But has the constant hyperactive thinker that most addicts have tried to still been quieted by meetings and basic step work? Rarely. We may be content to be living productive sober lives but the inability to quiet the noise in our heads leaves us with a sense of incompleteness. We've all heard that the programs suggest that we can be "happy, joyous and free" but if we're honest, most would admit they have a long way to go to reach that level of serenity.

As the eleventh step suggests, prayer and meditation are key tools to expanding the quality of our recovery to a higher paradigm. There is a good reason why the program includes a step that recommends we make meditation and prayer an active part of our daily life. Meditation has been the time-honored tool of choice to discipline and still the busy mind. For thousands of years in just about every culture, meditation practice has been used as a basic tool to achieve inner peace.

In working with those who want to start meditating, I've repeatedly heard the same complaint. "I'm not sure I can be a meditator because my mind is too busy." I usually just smile and reflect back to the person that their attempt at meditation is just revealing how chaotic their mind already is, and that's precisely the reason to meditate. I also suggest that when they sit to meditate, they don't need to get the mind to be quiet; they just need to watch the mind as it jumbles along and surrender what they are experiencing. My standard suggestion is to "just watch the rabbit pop out of the hole, run across the field and down into another hole." All one needs to do is just be the watcher. Nothing needs to be done with the movie that our mind is playing. Our only task is to be still and just watch and surrender the movie. Meditation is that simple.

Once one has become adept at just watching the movie as it unfolds across the screen of one's mind, it's possible to refine the meditative process a bit further. The classic method recommended in almost all meditation disciplines is to just watch the in-breath, allowing all else to fade into the background. Over time, as one's regular practice matures, the amount of mental noise experienced will become less and less, allowing us to experience a deeper sense of peace and relaxation, as the consequence of our practice.

There are thousands of books on how to meditate, but they all boil down to slowly disciplining the mind by just watching the breath. It really makes little difference if we have our eyes open or shut, or we sit in a chair or cross-legged on the floor. It makes little difference if we practice for a few minutes or for hours. What matters is that we just become quiet, allow the mind to do its thing as we simply watch and surrender the mind's content. Over time, as we regularly follow the simple practice of just surrendering the mind's chatter and noise, we will notice that the stream of material activity playing across the screen of the mind will start to slow down. This is unlikely to happen when we first start to practice. It took years for our minds to descend into chaos and will take time to reverse the process. We just need to sit patiently and watch. We don't have to make the thinker slow down; it will slow down on its own if we are not feeding it with additional inputs. Just like a puppy, if there isn't any engagement from us, it will become bored and tend to just curl up and go to sleep.

While there really isn't any wrong way

to meditate there are a few common helpful suggestions. It's recommended that we make our meditation 'good in the beginning, good in the middle and good at the end.' This simply suggests that we hold in mind an intention for our practice before we start, that we simply be the watcher while we are meditating, and offer thanks after our practice. It's also suggested that no matter how or where we choose to sit, we sit with our backs straight and erect to allow the free flow of energies up and down our chakras.

If one couples these two simple suggestions with a regular practice, one will quickly find a slowing of the over-active mind and a growing sense of relaxation. The term for this simple but profound payoff of regular meditation is captured by the word contemplation. As our practice becomes a way of life we will start to find ourselves less caught up in the mental noise of daily life. Like being the watcher during our sitting meditation, we will now start to be a watcher of things as they unfold as we go through our day. We will start to slow down, think less and watch more. Our practice of surrendering what we experience during sitting meditation will start to translate into being better able to surrender the challenging things that happen in our day. This is what is called adopting a contemplative lifestyle. Our regular sitting meditation has made it possible to adopt a slower and more mindful way of being throughout the day.

The subject of prayer can be a thorny one for many in recovery. Many come into recovery with conflicted feelings about the reality of a Higher Power, the value of prayer, the rightful place of religion, and the meaning of the word spiritual. We have all likely heard this confusion and the conflicting opinions expressed around the room when any of the various aspects of this subject surfaces. Resolving these conflicts is an essential element of reaching emotional and spiritual recovery

Like starting with any leg of the elephant will eventually lead you to the whole elephant, we can begin to unscramble these conflicts by starting anywhere. Let's start with religions. Religions are organizations committed to following the teachings of their founders. As such, most religions are committed to teaching the essence of spirituality and how to live a spiritual life. Unfortunately, there are many aspects of religions as organizations that have little to do with spirituality. Another way of stating this truth: spirituality is of a higher paradigm than any religion.

Spirituality is about what all the Avatars who founded the great religions experienced at the very top of the mountain. These exceedingly evolved beings experienced a Oneness with Divinity, and passed many Truths down to their followers. It was their followers who subsequently codified these teachings, forming a religion. The core Teachings of all these great Avatars are basically the same. They all experienced and taught their followers that Divinity was the ultimate Truth, Kindness, Compassion, Love, Wisdom, Impartiality and Forgiveness. These core understandings about Divinity and the nature of all things were central to all great religions at the time of their origination.

Unfortunately, the followers of these great Avatars were not as evolved as their Teachers, and as they recorded and passed on the teachings, they often contaminated them with their own opinions, and created dogmas and doctrines that started to deviate significantly from the essence of the original Teachings. This gradually watered down, and sometimes even inverted, the Truth of those Teachings.

Some religions have fared better than others

over time. For example, Mahayana Buddhism has changed very little since its inception in the time of the Buddha. At its core and throughout all of its literature is the simple statement, "This is offered that all beings may be freed from suffering and the roots of suffering and that they may find happiness and the roots of happiness." The core Teaching is simply to live one's life in a way that will bring happiness and relieve suffering to all beings. Not bad, not bad at all.

Unfortunately, over the centuries, some religions have been badly contaminated by power struggles and the introduction of new doctrines and dogmas, which were manifestations of the disturbed thinking of some members. These new dictums had nothing to do with the original Teaching and often were just the opposite to what the founder taught. The fallout from these aberrant teachings has led to religious wars, strife, and the slaughter of millions.

So where is it safe for the recovering person to seek spiritual guidance and wisdom? Traditionally, the world's great religions have been the repository of the wisdom of their founder. In addition, there are now many sources available that reflect the original spiritual wisdom of the great Avatars without being involved with a formal religion. We are blessed with many choices, but we must choose wisely. Any religion or literature, from whatever source, that is based on and teaches us to embrace Truth, Love, Wisdom, Kindness, Compassion, Impartiality and Forgiveness is a valid well from which to drink. Any religion, or organization or teaching that does otherwise should be avoided.

The majority of those in the programs have had at least some experience, as part of a formal religion, usually in their youth. Some are still involved with, and actively practicing that religion. Many regularly attended religious services and followed practices of regular prayer and service. Many who had been away from the religion of their youth during their years of active addiction had returned to re-engage with their religion. Most seem comfortable that these involvements constitute having an active prayer life as recommended by the 11th Step.

What about those who don't have a religious affiliation to help them create a prayer life? Does one need the formula prayers and practice of a religion to create an effective prayer life? Absolutely not. Just like in our discussion about meditation, prayer is really a simple process, even more simple than just being the watcher in meditation. Prayer is simply communicating with whatever we understand to be our Higher Power. It's that simple. No format or location or position or mode of dress is required. That having been said, many programs recommend the simple act of kneeling in the morning to ask for a day of abstinence, and kneeling in the evening to express gratitude for a day of sobriety to be helpful. The process is as simple as just opening one's heart to connect to the Ultimate Source of Love, Kindness, Wisdom, Truth, Compassion, Impartiality and Forgiveness.

Many in recovery like to use the "Third Step Prayer" from the "**Big Book**," or the "Prayer of St. Francis." There is no shortage of wonderful prayers in common use with which to talk to one's Higher Power. For a growing portion of the recovering community traditional formal prayers have been supplemented or even replaced by establishing an informal dialog style of prayer. Many see their Higher Power as their best friend and simply open their hearts as if they were chatting with their best buddy. As one member put it, "Man's best friend spelled backwards is still doG."

I'm personally attracted to the practice of writing a simple statement of petition to one's Higher Power. It can capture the essence of how one would like to communicate with their Best Friend.

Once the prayer has been committed to memory it can be said, not only morning and evening, but at random times across the day. Simply sitting at a stop light in traffic can become a moment of prayerfulness.

To give an example of a personal prayer, here's one I wrote years ago. When I first wrote it, I may have said it three or four times a day. Over time, that number has steadily increased to the point that now the prayer is the most natural thing to pop into my mind at an idle moment. These moments in the past would have been filled with ego chatter, but now have become periods of prayerful surrender. The prayer contains three elements of petition to my Higher Power. It's a request to free me from the bondage of the ego, a desire to live a life of Loving service and the willingness to surrender all the vanities of the ego. As a management consultant might put it, it's my mission statement.

"Come Holy Spirit, fill my heart with Love and Compassion, free me from the bondage of the ego so that I may more effectively serve as an instrument of Thy Truth.

I dedicate my life to the Loving service to all beings, that they may be freed from suffering and the roots of suffering, and may find happiness and the roots of happiness.

I humbly surrender all aspects of thinking, feeling, opinion, judgment, belief, perception and positions that may in any way interfere with an unobstructed Realization of Divinity. Not my will but Thy will be done."

That may appear long but it clearly states how I'd like to position my boat in the river. It's also long enough to periodically get me to slow down and create a break from the constant chatter of the ego.

I also have a few ultra-simple ways of praying. I carry a smooth three-sided gem stone in my pocket that's pleasant to hold with the fingers. As my day unfolds, instead of having to listen to the stories my mind is always trying to play I can just hold the stone and say, "I surrender," or "This moment is perfect and complete," or "Lord have Mercy" over and over and over. This simple form of prayer has never failed to buy me some relief from my over-active mind.

If you decide you'd like to have a prayer that captures the essence of how you'd like to regularly petition your best Friend, consider writing one of your own. Each one of us following the recovery road may be different but our spiritual needs are very similar. What the wise ones have suggested to be the high road to serenity is clearly marked. Prayer is the best way to access the power necessary for the journey.

SPONSORS

I don't think too many people would venture into the wilderness without a qualified guide. The journey into recovery is no different. Those who have lived under the yoke of an addiction, or with an active addict for that matter, have all lost their sense of perspective and grasp on reality. As they attempt to regain their sanity, the journey into recovery can be disconcerting and fraught with situations that can easily derail the process. Having a capable sponsor is essential.

For those well established in the program who are looking to improve the quality of their recovery, very few activities can be more rewarding and expansive than being a sponsor. As we've already discussed, Loving service is a core part of how all the 12 Step programs accomplish their miracles. Walking side by side with a newcomer may be the purest form of service. That said, for service to be effective for both the sponsor and the person they are trying to assist, it needs to be done prudently.

In the early days of AA, when there was no long term sobriety, anyone who had been in the rooms and abstinent for even a few weeks was considered capable of being a sponsor. Anyone who had been to a meeting before was quite qualified to stand at the door and say welcome to anyone who showed up for the meeting. Fortunately, today, all of the recovery programs have a cadre of members who have not only been in the rooms for a long time but have walked the walk necessary to have been restored to sanity.

Unfortunately, I've seen members with minimal recovery time raise their hand as someone willing to serve as a sponsor. I'm not sure that's wise for them, and could be problematic for anyone who might choose them as a sponsor. There's a sage program saying, "You can't give away what you haven't got." Until one has successfully ventured through the steps and reached a place where they can honestly say they are comfortable in their program, it's best they not attempt to guide others.

The danger of taking someone on to sponsor before one is ready is that it's most often an ego trip. Being a sponsor should not be about what the sponsor gains from the process, but about the desire to give back to the program what one has received out of a sense of deep gratitude. People with insufficient time in the program are unlikely to intuitively grasp this key distinction.

A truly effective sponsor will be available, patient, Loving and able to give clear feedback. The disease of addiction manifests quite differently in people, so every newcomer needs to be supported from a stance of flexibility. In being a sponsor it's best to recognize that serving as a sponsor can't be approached from the perspective of "one size fits all." Yes, there are core principles in helping people along the path, but they need to be taught with the recognition that not all newcomers will be able to absorb or utilize these tools at the same pace. Helping others from this sage perspective will benefit both parties.

AFFIRMATIONS

One of the most important life lessons we can learn is how much of a role attitude plays in how we experience life. How I attempt to see life has more to do with how I experience life than the details of one's life. In short, "Attitude Rules."

A book that makes this point with exceptional clarity is "**The Power of Intention**" by Dr. Wayne Dyer. Many readers may have seen Dr. Dyer present this in lecture form on Public TV. If you have not seen this presentation, it's well worth the effort to root it out from the Public TV archives and watch it. It contains life-changing insights.

Dr. Dyer and many other wise elders have expressed their belief that, "what we hold in mind tends to materialize." They assert that we are, in part, the author of what we experience in life. These may sound like crazy notions, but they are in fact validated by Quantum Mechanics and the advanced concepts underlying modern theoretical physics. The idea that how I think about something is an active part of what subsequently unfolds is not fantasy, but fact.

This being true, affirmations add impetus to those in recovery doing whatever they can to come at life with right thinking and a positive attitude. This reality is the basis for using wise sayings or positive statements that one repeats regularly, or simply holds in mind as a way of creating positive changes in one's life.

Most affirmations are short, simple and very focused statements, such as, "I am love." "I live in a world of simple abundance." "I choose to be kind at all times." Affirmations can be complex or simple, humorous or pithy, or aimed to help us get some traction in changing a habit. Here are a few that I've collected over the years. Many are the kind of statement that one puts on sticky notes in places where one can be reminded that they wish to incorporate this bit of wisdom into their daily life.

☐ There are only two things that exist: what is and my reaction to what is. I can't do anything about what is, but I can control my attitude.
☐ The opposite to the word nice is real.
☐ In order to see I must act.

- The need to be right is one of the most dangerous of human diseases.
- Balance is power.
- Every negative feeling I have is about the past.
- Ask 100% of the time for 100% of what you want and be willing to negotiate the difference.
- Forgiving is the best way of taking back my energy previously left in negative destructive events.
- Any problem that I'm handling is no longer a problem.
- The only way out is through.
- Our task is not to seek love, but to find what stands in the way of Love.
- When I take responsibility for what I've created, I can change it.
- My serenity is inversely proportional to my expectations.
- Certainty is the enemy of Truth.
- All of us contain within, the seeds of our own wellness.
- Most of our troubles in life stem from our unwillingness to embrace legitimate pain.
- Discovery is not going to new places but seeing where you are with new eyes.

- Nobody is afraid of the unknown; what we're afraid of is loss of the known.
- You can't heal what you can't feel.
- If all you have is a hammer everything starts to look like a nail.
- Anything we can truly feel, especially in the presence of an empathetic listener, becomes transformed and moves toward healing.
- Anything in our unconscious that is unresolved will be projected onto others or be acted out in ways that don't work for us.
- A life based on broken commitments simply does not work.

PHYSICAL WHOLENESS

To do justice to the need for and potential payoffs of rehabilitating the body of the recovering person would require a book of its own. The majority of those coming to a 12 Step program have suffered negative physical consequences along with the mental and spiritual bankruptcy that brought them for help. Going to meetings and working the steps does a lot to rehabilitate the mind and promote spiritual wellbeing but does little to restore the damage done to the body.

The term "Physical Wholeness" is meant to be all inclusive, ranging from activities like Yoga, Tai Chi, weight and aerobic workouts to therapeutic massage, proper diet and general life style improvements. All these modalities have a place in the recovery process and, in my experience, those who have added a good number of these elements into their program have manifested a more joyful and serene level of recovery.

To address each of these items or areas in any depth would double the size of this book. Suffice it to say that anyone who really wants to create quality physical recovery needs to investigate and embrace many of these modalities. Each has a payoff ranging from the release of calming endorphins to better weight control. The body is designed to be well and has within it the seeds of its own wellness. No matter how much damage the disease has done to an addict's body, simple Loving care and incorporation of these supportive tools will usually pay handsome dividends.

I do think special mention should be given to the importance of improved nutrition for all those who wish the best possible level of recovery. As a society, we have really devolved in our dietary habits and this is doubly so for those with addictive disease. Compulsive eating has become more common than alcoholism. Many addicts who become abstinent from drugs and alcohol find themselves switching their addictive needs to the calming effects of food substances. Eating disorders are now at epidemic levels in our culture.

I will not attempt to cover the spectrum and impact of eating and nutritional disorders. There are great resources available to do that. Additionally, I won't attempt to provide guidance as to what should be in a healthy diet because that information is also readily available. I'm especially fond of "**Eating Well for Optimum Health**" by Andrew Weil, MD. Dr. Weil has a gift for making the complex quite easy to understand and is a wonderful mix of modern medical wisdom and old fashioned common sense. In addition to referring the reader to Dr. Weil, I would like to offer a few ideas about how to eat in a healthy manner. These ideas can apply for any person, any place, and any time.

(1) Find out what are the right foods and food amounts your body needs to maintain an appropriate weight for your level of activity, body build, and genetic make-up.

(2) Decide on when you should eat, set up a routine, and eat at those times. Eat by the clock, not because you're hungry, but because it's time to eat.

(3) Learn to disappear hunger. Unless one is dealing with a starvation scenario, hunger will usually disappear in about 20 minutes after onset, if you ignore its presence.

(4) Avoid eating between meals or just because you're hungry.

(5) Put a sign on the refrigerator and food panty cabinet door that says "ADULTS ONLY."

(6) If these simple ideas don't work: Call OA.

JOURNALING

The process that most people now call journaling, over the centuries has been termed spiritual writing. It isn't about keeping a log of daily activities. It's about having a place where we can unwind our thoughts and feelings and potentially gain perspective. It's a method that helps uncover what's really going on inside. The attempt to use such a tool to explore our inner world is the very essence of the emotional and spiritual quest.

It's important to remember that we function at two levels: our ego's animal nature and our non-linear essence which is spirit. The challenge of diminishing the power and scope of the ego's hold on our lives and gaining a deeper understanding of what we truly are as spiritual beings is at the core of all the recovery programs. One of the most effective tools in monitoring this process as it unfolds is regular journaling.

The process is quite simple. One just needs a

place to record one's thoughts, and the habit to regularly sit and unload whatever is crossing one's mind into that receptacle. It's best that the place one is using to record one's inner thoughts be secure from being read by others. Having a secure journal helps us relax and be willing to write our most intimate thoughts and feelings. There was a time when the only thing available for this was a pen and a paper journal. Now, with the wide variety of electronic tools available there are many options.

To be most useful, the process needs to be integral to one's everyday life. The more often one journals, the deeper the depths that will be reached by the process. The deeper one journeys into the inner world, the greater the reward.

The reason journaling is such an effective tool is quite simple. When one sits and starts to write, the first things to flow into the journal will be the thoughts central to the ego as it attempts to control what will happen in the near future. That's standard fare for the ego—looking ahead to make sure the path is safe. As one continues to write, the ego's agenda will soften and deepen, and more intuitive material from our less conscious awareness starts to show up on the page. As one becomes adept at the process and more relaxed, one will often find that things about themselves will show up on the page that they hadn't really known or understood before they started to write. Journaling is a very simple, direct way to start to unlock what's stored in that Pandora's box we call the unconscious.

I can't stress enough how effective this tool can be in unscrambling the fur ball that's the normal mental state for most addicts in recovery. The dark energy of things that led to the addiction and things that happened as the result of the addictive process are still stored in the software of the unconscious. Unscrambling all that crossed wiring takes time, patience and effective tools. Journaling is a very effective tool.

TALKING THERAPY

A time-honored adjunct recovering addicts have used to climb out of the rut associated with their disease has been to spend time sorting through their issues with an empathetic listener. In the early days this was usually a sponsor or a member of the clergy. In the last few decades the recovering community has had available trained professionals who understand the disease, many from personal experience, and who have undergone professional training in how to support the recovering person clear the wreckage of their past.

There isn't a huge difference between what is offered by a therapist and what can be accomplished with diligent application of the 12 steps with the support of a good sponsor. In fact, for a number of years I taught a graduate school course entitled, "The convergence of traditional psychotherapies and the 12 steps of the recovery programs." It was my contention that psychotherapy without doing step work as well was usually ineffective, but supportive psychotherapy can be a great adjunct to those working the steps because they are really utilizing the same psychological principles.

After many decades of doing psychotherapy with recovering addicts in an office practice, I can attest to the truth of the above assertion. Sustained abstinence from all addictive substances and behaviors, active attendance at meetings, a good sponsor and home group, working the steps and supportive psychotherapy usually will result in most recovering addicts finding a new balance, clearing out some of the more difficult bits of wreckage from their past and so usher in a contented sobriety. I think it's safe to say that this combination has been the Gold Standard for the recovery process in recent years. Not everyone in recovery needs psychotherapy but few with addictive disease would not profit from some professional help in sorting out some of their more complex life issues.

Unfortunately, even the highest quality talking therapy, be it from a licensed counselor, psychologist, or psychiatrist cannot get to the root of many of the issues that keep the recovering addict from achieving true emotional wellbeing. A significant portion of the recovering community carries the burden of deeply rooted post-traumatic stress disorder and other emotional consequences of their pre-recovery years. Many of these disorders have been highly resistant to the best program and psychological treatment approaches, and as a result, the most recent approach has been to add psychotropic medications to the mix.

As a physician, I understand and have prescribed such medications for recovering addicts when necessary. Unfortunately, I have always felt they were being over prescribed by many of my peers, and are being used as a Band-Aid to save the time and expense associated with more time consuming, non-pharmacologic treatments. It is important to note that I'm not talking about recovering addicts with psychosis, manic depressive disorder and endogenous (genetic) depression. These are biologically based disorders and require a biological resolution with the use of appropriate medication. In my experience, though, this group only constitutes a small percentage of those in the recovering community who for one reason or another have been medicated by the medical community.

Do these medications work? I do think they can help most people achieve a more comfortable existence. Unfortunately, they do little or nothing to resolve the underlying issues that lead to their being prescribed in the first place. To me, it's like regularly taking an antacid but continuing to eat foods that you know cause you heartburn. Antacids may work but the cause of the problem is unaffected. In my experience, most members of the recovering community who are prescribed medications fall under the same rubric. The medications may help, but the underlying causes remain unresolved unless they are given meaningful attention.

Do we have sufficiently cost-effective and readily available tools that can help recovering persons deal with the deeper emotional issues most carry into recovery? Not really. Until recent years, there has been a significant shortfall of good options, but that's changing. Many of these new therapies are still in their infancy, and the majority are still little known, or not yet readily available in many locations. Yet, their promise in offering true resolution to sufferers who have up to now had little hope of achieving emotional wellness is well-documented.

EXPRESSIVE THERAPIES

One of the lesser known or talked about but more effective therapeutic tools is the use of the expressive arts to unlock things trapped in the deeper psyche. Standing in front of a canvas and just letting whatever one feels flow onto the canvas is a prime example. Note this is similar to the journaling process. Writing poetry or engaging in expressive movement fall into the rubric. In fact, something as simple as having a collection of small flat stones on a desk that one rearranges in new creative patterns each day is the same. The key to this form of healing is to just step up, let go, and allow intuition to play out whatever wants to come to the surface.

This may sound easy, but it's not. In my experience, the overwhelming majority of those entering recovery are emotionally as tight as a drum and struggle to let go of anything. "We leave claw marks." That was one of the reasons we used an addictive behavior or substance to relax and unwind in the first place. Taking away the modifying effects of an addiction usually reveals the underlying emotional patterns in spades. Abstinence, meetings, and step work usually help but the core emotional rigidity of the ego structure tends to persist.

When these uncomfortable emotional patterns are sufficiently bothersome, many seek help from a therapist. As we discussed above, the talking therapies can be helpful but have their limitations. Fortunately, recent studies have demonstrated that simply adding expressive tools to our recovery process will slowly start breaking down the ego's strong grip, and bring trapped material to the surface. Like journaling, the use of this simple tool slips below the surface and helps unlock the painful trapped material that our psyche is working so hard to keep contained.

The general experience of those who have utilized art as part of their recovery tools has been that what shows up on the canvas is often material that will not be easily accessed consciously until some future time. There may be clues about blocked memories or unrecognized strong feelings that the conscious mind does not yet feel safe enough to allow to surface. The simple act of expressing this trapped material on the canvas starts to bleed off energy and make it safer for the mind to surface the issue to where it can be processed and resolved.

The key awareness is that many of those coming into recovery, for whatever reason, are sitting on a powder keg of repressed material. One either finds ways of safely surfacing and resolving that material, or it will have repressive effects on the quality of one's recovery. A very gentle and effective way of softening the explosive energy is to dissipate some of that energy through expressive activities.

BODY WORK

Getting a massage has long been honored as a way of relieving tension and promoting wellbeing. The fact that massage has been practiced as a healing art in most cultures for thousands of years validates its value.

What has not been well understood, even by many massage practitioners, is the underlying aspect of the massage process that results in improved wellbeing. Each massage tradition has its own mythology as to how the benefits are transmitted to the recipient, but recent insights suggest there is much more at work than has been understood by these traditions.

As we have suggested in many places throughout this book, attractor fields, as postulated by Non-Linear Dynamics, are a silent, unrecognized, underlying force in much of the universe. The massage process is a good example of this reality. The recipient has their skin and muscles stroked and manipulated in a way that makes them relax and experience a sense of relief. A simple mechanism: soothing hands press on various parts of the body and the body relaxes. But is this all that's going on? Hardly.

There are many high energy attractor fields conferring healing energy during a massage. One of the most obvious is the very act of someone intending to provide a healing modality to another human. This is similar to what all 12 Step meeting participants experience from each other by merely attending a meeting. When a healer of any sort, be they surgeon, psychologist, or massage therapist does what they have been trained to do in the service of another human, they confer a strong healing energy to the person they are treating. This is present and almost as important as anything they actually do physically in the session.

Another more recently recognized aspect of massage is the release of trapped negative energy within the body. While it's true that we record our life experiences in the software we call memory, an additional significant mechanism is the emotional energy nodules we store in the physical body. As the massage proceeds, and the muscles are Lovingly manipulated these trapped energies start to be released. This understanding is significant because as we have discussed, talk therapies rarely get to the stored root of emotional distress. Deep Tissue massage seems to be able to do just that.

All of the different massage techniques can help the body to release stored energy. Be it Reflexology, Shiatsu, Deep Tissue massage, Reiki, or any of the other common massage styles practiced, they all help to mobilize trapped emotional energy. Unfortunately, that this energy release is happening, and how to take advantage of what's unfolding is usually ignored. People see their session as body work and miss the fact that the very act of undergoing a massage is presenting them with the opportunity to experience, release, and process previously repressed emotional energy. A simple way to take advantage of what's released would be, after the massage to then take one's self to a quiet place and journal for a while.

I'm not suggesting that getting a massage needs to be turned into a psychotherapy session. On the other hand it is important to be aware that the experience has the potential to open emotional doors and presents an opportunity to take another small step toward freedom of the spirit.

The importance of adding ways we might

process the energy being released from a massage isn't unique to body work. A number of the other techniques we have already discussed and will address in the next few sections present the same golden opportunity. The combination of various modalities is usually more effective than using just one tool. They seem to be synergistic and enhance each other when used in combination. I like to call it the "dig 'em up, move 'em out" method. When we find ways of dislodging the trapped energies and combine that with methods that can effectively process what has been surfaced, we are on the fast track to an ever increasing level of serene sobriety.

BREATH WORK

Doing Breath-work may have saved my life back in the mid 80's. I had lived through the fighting in Vietnam and with the help of active participation in the 12 Step process, had been able to function well for over a decade after my return. And then things started to come apart mentally and I was plunged into a very dark place. I now know the meaning of the phrase "Dark Night of the Soul." My battle with PTSD had just begun and was to be far from a one-night affair.

Fortunately, I knew a very gifted and Loving psychiatrist and enlisted his help. Eddy felt I would make better progress if I was not put on a supportive medication. He also strongly suggested I increase my attendance at meetings. I saw Eddy weekly but the darkness in which I was swimming only deepened over the months. My effectiveness in my work and as a husband and father really suffered. Over the next few years, despite Eddy's best efforts to help me start to unlock the emotional pain that was destroying my life, I continued to sink even deeper into depression and the terror of my PTSD memories. Eddy still felt that I would have a better chance of breaking free from my malaise if I stayed off medication.

Then Eddy made a suggestion which I think may well have saved my life. He had heard of a new technique called Holotropic Breathwork®. This technique was said to be able to help unlock and release trapped emotional material. We agreed, in addition to our weekly talking sessions, that I would also come weekly to give this new modality a try.

Over the next year, I went to his office every Monday morning. I would lie on a mat on the floor and Eddy would take me through a relaxation sequence. I would then start to breathe deeply and more deeply and more rapidly till I went into a sustained hyperventilation state. The first few sessions doing this for over an hour led to tingling in my limbs but not much else. However, by the third session, once in the sustained deep breathing state, I started to make guttural noises and my body would experience involuntary movements.

By the 4th or 5th session, I started to feel the

stirrings of anger. Up until that session, I had been unable to access the rage and other emotions that both Eddy and I knew were trapped in my body. As the series of sessions progressed, I wasn't exactly sure who or what I was angry at, but the rage poured out of me. This went on for months and as the time passed and a wide array of repressed emotions surfaced, my mood started to lighten and my ability to function improved.

My recollection of that year and the years that followed are of a steady uphill climb to process the material the sessions had released. How that all unfolded isn't important to the discussion of breath-work. What is important is that in the deep throes of depression, precipitated by overwhelming PTSD, and without the use of any psychotropic medications, I was able to break the trapped dark energy loose with this technique. I'm not sure how long I could have gone on the way I was experiencing life if I hadn't been offered the opportunity to do breath-work. When I read the statistics that, on average, 22 combat veterans commit suicide every day I say with the deepest gratitude, "There but for the Grace of God, go I."

I know that's a long prologue to introducing this modality, but I know of no better way to make the point. Even with the best traditional therapeutic tools in the hands of a very gifted therapist, and in someone who was living the 12 Step life, there were emotional burdens that were immoveable. Far too many of my military peers are still living deep in the woods emotionally, or on the streets. Far too many have committed suicide. Far too many marriages have failed. Far too many still live with trapped memories that terrorize their dreams and contaminate their efforts to live normal lives. Breath-work saved me from that.

So what is this modality? Fortunately, we now have access to an abundance of authentic information on the web. Between topic specific YouTube presentations and TED talks, we even have easy access to the people who originated a new tool. Such is the case with breath-work.

The doctor whose work led to what is now known worldwide as Holotropic Breathwork® is Stanislav Grof, MD. Just Google his name and you will find a cornucopia of material about the technique, the theories behind how it works, and how it can be used to help relieve human emotional burdens. With such a wealth of first-hand information on the subject, I will defer to Dr. Grof and let him talk about it all in his own words.

The number of therapists being trained in offering breath-work is rapidly expanding. Breath-work is being offered in two different ways. One is the classic Holotropic Breathwork® experience which is usually done as a multiple day, small group process event with the individual's breath-work sessions being two to three hours long accompanied by loud, evocative music, and followed by the opportunity to process the material surfaced by creating a mandala and group sharing. Unfortunately, these classic three day experiences are not readily available in all geographic regions and are somewhat expensive. The good news is these sessions, if you can access one, are extremely powerful and usually surface material that takes months or years to process with more traditional modalities, so attendance at these longer sessions can in fact save both time and money.

The other much more common and readily available method is done in a traditional office setting with the sessions usually lasting a few hours. The therapists who utilize this technique often incorporate a variety of other modalities into the sessions, but the core of the process is what I did with Eddy back in the 80's, and has the ability to release trapped emotional energy by following the breath into the deeper recesses of the psyche.

EMDR AND CBT

The health care professions have so many complex names for things that it's tended to abbreviate the titles for diseases and treatments. Of course, we now have the people who write advertisements doing the same thing, so much so that ads have become a world of alphabet soup. So I apologize for shortening the names for these two very important treatments. Eye Movement Desensitization Reflex and Cognitive Behavioral Therapy sessions are part of the new current gold standard treatments for post-traumatic stress disorder (PTSD)

We most often associate PTSD with those who have experienced war, sexual violation, natural disasters and other horrific events. In reality, modern society is a fertile ground for the production of every day events that result in the emotional response called PTSD in some people. Those who find their way into 12 Step programs are more likely to carry the symptoms associated with this syndrome than the general population. In my experience, a high percentage of those who experienced periodic relapses or developed an alternative addiction did so in an attempt to manage unresolved symptoms of PTSD.

The 12 steps are well suited to helping the recovering addict sort out and cope with their addiction and the associated emotional baggage. Unfortunately for the vast majority of those with PTSD in good active recovery, the symptoms of the syndrome are only dampened, but not relieved by the recovery process. The ongoing underlying angst resulting from unresolved emotional trauma is what keeps many in recovery from realizing true freedom of the spirit. Until we find a way to relieve the inner pressure of the trapped energy from old emotional trauma, we are not able to experience true serenity. If we want to live a life of recovery where we can truly say we are "happy, joyous and free," we need to find a way of clearing the wreckage of the past, all of it.

The search for ways to root out trapped emotional energies has always been the Holy Grail of the mental health profession. The search for answers in the 19th century resulted in the development of the fields of psychiatry and psychology. There are great libraries filled with numerous books positing different methods of achieving this goal—and most of what is presented has achieved little more than what those who work the 12 steps accomplish on their own. Until recent years the psychiatric and psychological professions found they could only get so far in relieving emotional suffering which led them to searching for cures with medication. We have already noted that has been, at best, a cost effective Band-Aid approach. Then along came CBT and a bit later, EMDR.

Other than what I'm about to discuss now, everything I've written in this book is material that I learned in depth at 12 Step meetings or in my years of clinical practice. Unfortunately, I have no first-hand experience with either EMDR or CBT therapy other than what I've read, reports from peers, and my interface with people in the program who have undergone treatment with these modalities. Additionally, I've found the web has a wide array of quality presentations by experienced experts that can lay out the theory behind, and the methods used in, both these modalities. I suggest the reader check out those resources for details. I will confine my further discussion to fleshing out a bit more about what these modalities are trying to accomplish.

As I discussed previously, we store emotional trauma as trapped energy in the physical body. One single emotional trauma experience, once stored as an energy nodule, can subsequently generate many layers of thoughts stacked layer upon layer. The longer we keep replaying the memory of the event, the more layers of material about the event get stacked up. Remembering the event, and some of the stack of accompanying memories about the event, gets stuck in our psyche and just keeps going around and around and around like an old phonograph record with a scratch. These memories are in a well-developed groove. How to get the memory unstuck has always been the problem. Enter CBT and EMDR. In both therapies the key to creating relief is getting at the root energy and transforming that energy into new memories. One can visualize this as surfacing and rewriting mental software to replace the old corrupt mental programs which had become stuck. The techniques to get the old material unstuck is done primarily though focused reprograming techniques during CBT sessions.

With the development of EMDR, an added tool

has become available to augment the reprogramming discussion techniques of CBT. It was discovered that using a variety of strategies to get the patients to move their eyes from side to side resulted in the trapped emotional material becoming uprooted and subsequently, more easily reprogrammed. I'm really not sure how eye movement pulls the rabbit out of the hat, but it does. Both techniques have shown some success in reprogramming a painful old memory into a positive new memory, thereby reducing the angst associated with the recollection of the traumatic event.

Both these modalities are about resolving painful emotional material. Do they work? I think the most honest answer is reasonably well for many people. The outcome studies for these modalities report that the everyday traumas of growing up, failed social interactions, illnesses et al., do respond well.

Unfortunately, there is a subset of PTSD that is so painful and powerfully imbedded that even these two significant tools have not always been able adequately to get the old energy nodule unstuck sufficiently to allow for successful processing and reprograming. Combat veterans, survivors of torture, recurrent sexual abuse, and similar massive emotional insult survivors have been resistant to most treatments. A good percentage of this category of survivor can and do achieve long, satisfying abstinence within the supportive structure of the recovery process but unfortunately their inner world is nowhere close to being at peace, much less, serene.

There are newer treatments being studied that have shown remarkable success in relieving the distress of even the most severe PTSD sufferer. I will discuss these new treatments in a later section.

WISDOM TRADITION SPIRITUALITY

All of the 12 Step programs make clear that, at their core, they are spiritual programs. Unfortunately, very few members can give a clear explanation of what this means, and even fewer have mined the depth of what's available to truly live a spiritual life in recovery.

To truly grasp what being spiritual means, it is helpful to go back to Bill Wilson's statement that the program was all about "deflation of ego at depth." What Bill was suggesting was that the core of the program was focused on defusing the human ego's importance as the centerpiece of who we think we are and the driver of our choices. This concept was not new with Bill. Freeing us from the power of the ego has been at the root of all the great Wisdom Traditions in every culture over thousands of years. They all had as their focus the same goal: the deflation of the human ego at depth.

No matter if it was Buddhism, Christianity, Islam, Judaism, Hinduism, or some of the lesser known, more obscure disciplines, all agree that the root of all human suffering can be traced to the ego and its survival strategies. Each of these traditions has taught various ways of taming and overcoming the power of the ego.

Each of these traditions was founded by a man who, by whatever means, was able to completely transcend the ego, and Realize what they truly were at the core of their being. They were able to experience the Oneness of all things. They were able to realize that, at the core of our being, we are all an unblemished manifestation of Divinity. They were all able to realize absolute freedom from human emotional suffering. They were able to realize that while their physical bodies might be corruptible, their being, in Oneness with Divinity, was eternal. They were able to realize that Divinity wasn't just transcendent—up there, but Imminent—within, as the essence of all things. Over the centuries, in all of these traditions there have been men and women who have also been able to transcend the human ego and have reaffirmed the original teachings. These evolved beings have been referred to as Mystics and Sages.

What has the 10,000 plus year history of the world's Wisdom Traditions to do with achieving serenity? The simple answer is they are the world's repository of information on how best to overcome the ego at depth. All of these traditions, despite much of the religious dogmas and rules created by their followers over time, have at their core, sage advice and proven tools to help members become progressively freed from the bondage of the ego, and to experience a quiet mind and serene sobriety.

The problem with the core information available from most of these traditions is the material was written in another language, in a different culture and in a different era, all of which has made it difficult for most of us to understand what's been offered. Yes, there are translations available and books that do a reasonable job in making this material understandable. Yet most of it remains abstract. Fortunately, the occurrence of true Sages and Mystics has not been limited to the distant past. In every age and in most cultures, there have been people freed from the limitations of the ego and this has continued to this day.

It is important to recognize that not every guru and baba that claims to be enlightened is the real deal. In fact, the world has always been full of false prophets. While it may be hard to separate the real from the phony, a simple litmus test should help decide who's the real deal and who is a fraud. The best criterion is this: "By their fruits you shall know them." The truly spiritual, advanced teachers will manifest Love, Compassion, Kindness, Forgiveness, Impartiality, Humility, as well as teach a Wisdom that resonates to the very core of one's being as Truth.

Our age has been blessed with many such Teachers of Truth. Wayne Dyer, Eckhart Tolle, David Hawkins, Rupert Spira and Byron Katie are just a few of the wise, gifted English-speaking teachers whose messages have the potential to help us loosen the bondage of the ego, and allow us to experience a greater sense of inner peace. While there are books available by these various teachers, the web has their teachings abundantly available, free of charge.

For those who want more than just contented sobriety, venturing into the study of the Wisdom Traditions as passed on by these gifted teachers is a super highway to the goal of reducing the ego's power so that we can better live a life that is "happy, joyous and free."

SACRED CHEMICALS

The field of psychiatry has been in decline for the past few decades. Insurance companies have been successful in restricting policy holders from being reimbursed for most psych services and very few people have the means to cover protracted therapy out of pocket. In addition, government and state regulations have progressively restricted what mental health professionals can do in serving the mentally ill. As a result, other than treatments for major psychiatric illnesses like schizophrenia, bi-polar illnesses, endogenous depression, and other severe chronic mental disorders, almost all psychiatric treatments have been reduced to the expediency of just medicating the symptoms. Little, if any, effort is made to permanently resolve the patient's underlying issues. We live in an era of Band-Aid therapies for emotional disorders.

The bottom line being that anyone with a chronic mental illness or carrying the horrific scars of severe

PTSD may not be able to gain access to effective treatment and is at risk of finding themselves living in a protracted state of emotional turmoil, or joining the homeless, wandering the streets and tunnels of our cities. What of the vast majority of the population who are still functioning well enough to have a roof over their head and money for food but who nevertheless suffer emotional disorders?

The current state of mental health services in the US is such that very, very few, if any, will find any treatment options available other than a community mental health clinic where they will be assessed and simply medicated. Just Band-Aid therapy. The treatment of mental illness in all the developed societies has degenerated to the point that even the most optimistic observer would have to admit things have reached a point where they are unacceptable. The problem is clear and change is required. The pregnant question, for a long while, has been, how are we to reinvent the system in ways that will be cost effective, humane, and readily available to all elements of society?

At the moment I see no shining lights signaling a new era, where there will be cost-effective, quality, comprehensive mental health services widely available. But if we step back I think we can identify that the void that's been created as traditional psychiatric and mental health services become hard to find, is starting to be filled by new creative treatments. The wide availability of the various 12 Step programs has played a major role in filling the void. We have also explored in previous sections a variety of new and creative treatments that show promise in helping to reduce emotional suffering. But clearly, this all falls short in addressing what is clearly a major unmet need for better treatment options.

As has always been true when there has been a crisis or a major unmet need, we humans have tapped into the innate creative capacity of the human mind. Thinking outside the box and venturing into unknown territory have often unearthed previously unimagined and inventive solutions. Today, we all enjoy the fruits of this ongoing process where crisis has led to unexpected rewards, not just to resolve the issue at hand, but far beyond. The psychiatric community is in desperate need of that type of creative revolution.

Many of the disease treatments currently in use by modern medicine are actually just updated refinements of treatments that have been in use since prehistoric days. The medicine men and women of primitive cultures with their plant medicines, have provided key insights to the pharmaceutical industry that have led to many of the sophisticated treatments in use today. Simply, the medicine-men and shamans of both ancient societies, as well as the primitive societies still in existence today, have had treatments that studies have shown, effected cures of emotional suffering currently not being achieved by modern medicine. These primitive but effective treatments have all involved a combination of both ritual and plant medicine. The use of psychedelic medicines in these cultures has been within both a religious context as well as a therapeutic context. Collectively, these medicines have been called "Sacred Chemicals" because of their effectiveness in relieving suffering.

Just as the pharmaceutical industry has already done in exploring primitive plants, medicines, and developing current therapies, there is a high probability that investigation of these Sacred Chemicals might lead to the discovery of more effective treatments of mental disorders. Very few people today are aware of the very exciting research that was done with LSD and other psychedelic drugs in the 1940's, 50's and 60's at prestigious institutions like Johns Hopkins and Harvard. The studies showed very promising results in a wide range of maladies that result in human mental suffering. A number of mental disorders were actually effectively eliminated with a series of treatments with these drugs. This was also true for the mentally healthy who were severely ill. Hospice patients who were exceedingly fearful of their impending death, given one or more treatments with LSD or psilocybin (magic mushrooms), showed dramatically reduced levels of fear, which allowed them to die in peace. There are many reports available in the medical literature about the benefits to be derived from therapeutic use of ibogaine, ayahuasca, and other similar herbal medicines. There is an abundance of information about these drugs on the web and in TED and YouTube presentations.

As a specialist in addiction medicine, my bias has been to lump psychedelic drugs in with all the other mind-altering drugs and behaviors used by addicts to cope. Certainly, anyone who lived through the 60's and 70's saw these agents used in many inappropriate ways. As a result of their over-the-top use during those years, the federal government banned all of these drugs, making them category one controlled substances, meaning that even hospitals and research facilities could no longer have access to the drugs, even for controlled research projects. Yes, there was a need in the 60's and 70's to control what was happening on the street with these chemicals but as usual in these matters, the government fixed a broken watch with boxing gloves.

In 1986 a group of mental health professionals formed an organization called MAPS, or Multidisciplinary Approach to Psychedelic Studies. It was their goal to take the necessary steps to get the government to again allow the study of these banned chemicals in hopes of finding a proper place for them in the treatment of mental illness, should they prove effective. Over the past thirty years they have reignited interest in this class of chemicals to the point that the government has again allowed their study. There are clinical trials in progress in many major institutions at this point including Harvard, Johns Hopkins, and the California Institute for Integral Studies, to name a few.

The early results of these studies have not only been exciting, but in some cases, have been truly remarkable. For example, in controlled studies of survivors of recurrent sexual abuse and combat veterans with the severest form of PTSD, whose symptoms had been resistant to all other treatments, with just three one-day treatments spread over three months using MDMA, the active ingredient in the outlawed drug Ecstasy, results showed dramatic relief in over 85% of those in the study. The results of these studies can be found on the MAPS website, as well as a wealth of information about the potential clinical value of other Sacred Chemicals in the treatment of mental disorders.

I still view this entire class of chemicals with an abundance of caution when they are being considered for therapeutic use by anyone in recovery. That said, having seen the ongoing angst carried by many people with long term recovery, who have been resistant to the currently available treatments, the early results of studies with these chemicals have caught my attention. Further studies are necessary, not only in how effective they are for various mental disorders, but also more specifically, their safety for use by recovering people with these disorders.

One point should be kept in mind as we watch these promising treatments go through the various hoops required before being available for general use. These drugs are really no different than any other medication currently approved for clinical use. A drug used as it was designed to be used usually produces positive outcomes. A drug used for recreational purposes, rather than the way it was intended, is almost always problematic. So far, across multiple controlled studies there has been no evidence that psychedelic drugs are addictive in nature. Of course, we all know addicts can find a way to become addicted to a glass of water.

HIGH OCTANE HELP

We all know the process of recovery is a "boots on the ground" process. We say, "Meeting makers make it." "We walk the walk." When people show up, good things tend to happen, not because of their efforts, but despite their efforts. When people show up, it is well said that "God is doing for us what we cannot do for ourselves."

Fortunately, over the decades, all of the various 12 Step communities have generated a body of literature that their members can tap into for inspiration and guidance. As we discussed in a previous section, most programs have a **"Big Book"** and many also have a **"Twelve and Twelve"** step book. These invaluable tools have been the bedrock of written guidance for the recovery communities.

There is also now available a wealth of non-conference approved literature that has also proven invaluable to program members. The wisdom and clarity of these tomes has made it possible for members to tap into material that has the potential to expand the depth and quality of their recoveries. The authors and books I've highlighted below are but a small fraction of what's available, but these books and authors, in my experience, seem to hold special attraction for those program members who appear to have achieved the highest states of serenity.

Scott Peck "The Road Less Traveled"

Very few books have sold as many copies as this book of sage wisdom. In fact, it's been so popular that it stayed for decades on the New York Times Best Seller List. It's easy to read and speaks very clearly of ways of understanding and conducting one's life in order to experience the greatest level of peace and joy. For many years, I used to give a copy to every new patient in my office practice. It's a must-read.

Stephen Covey "Seven Habits of Highly Effective People"

This book is the modern day equivalent of **"The Road Less Traveled."** It's become required reading in many college courses and I doubt anyone has been able to complete an MBA (Masters in Business Administration) without absorbing the lessons in this exceptional book. Covey is a very gifted, almost conversational writer who can translate even sometimes quite complex concepts into easily understood ideas. I personally found this book to be transformative, especially the fourth habit which encourages us to adopt a "Win-Win" posture. I had always seen the world as a place where there must be winners and losers. Covey taught me otherwise. Adopting this habit can be a real game changer.

Wayne Dyer **"The Power of Intention"**

Dyer is well known to most of us because of his wonderful presentations on National Public Television and various venues around the world. Perhaps his best known publication, **"The Power of Intention,"** is available both in book form and as a Public TV presentation. Dyer is a gifted presenter and exceptionally easy to understand. If you haven't seen this lecture give yourself a treat and watch it.

His presentation on intention is doubly important because it focuses our attention on the most powerful tool we humans possess, our ability to Intend. The Great Wisdom Traditions all teach two important points: the only thing we can know with any certainty is that we exist, and the only true freedom we have is the power of intention. This jibes very well with the quote heard throughout the halls— "I'm responsible for the effort but not for the results." In short, we can Intend and do the leg work, but must then trust Divinity to manifest an outcome that serves the greatest good.

Eckhart Tolle **"The Power of Now"**

This simple book is a great example of the reality that any book that is worthy of being widely read will not only find its way to the market but will be widely disseminated with or without advertisement. The book was published by a very small publisher and was not advertised when it was released. Yet, within a year, it was a bestseller in Canada, and soon after in the US, and now, around the world. It is styled to be used as a reflection guide with short, one or two page readings. The writing is simple and clear. Its thrust is to help us refocus on the reality that we can only live in the Now. This is just one of Tolle's books. His lectures are readily available on

YouTube as well as available for sale. This is a book one might choose to have on the table next to the bed as part of a morning or evening ritual or beside our meditation spot. The book is pure Wisdom.

"A Course in Miracles"

I've met many program people who have utilized the daily practices in this workbook to great effect. Its focus is to recontextualize how we perceive reality. It does this by asking one to read a daily lesson and follow the instructions related to the lesson across the day. Those who have done the daily lessons through a full year cycle claim it has been life-changing. The central theme of the book is Forgiveness of both self and others.

Andrew Weil, MD "Eating Well for Optimum Health"

Dr. Weil is a professor of Family Medicine at the University of Arizona who has written many books on wellness. His books teach how to heal ourselves without resorting to traditional medicine. They are a delightful mix of good science, folk medicine and common sense. All of his books are well worth reading, but his ideas about sane eating will be especially useful for those in recovery.

Pema Chodron **"The Pema Chodron Collection"**

Pema is a Buddhist Nun and the Abbess at a Buddhist monastery in Cape Breton, Nova Scotia. Before she became a nun, she was a wife and mother, which makes her blending of insights about how to cope with the realities of everyday life and Buddhist teaching especially effective. All of her books have been short, focused on how to better manage daily living, and easy to read. The "Collection" gathers her most popular offerings in one easy to handle book.

Robert Johnson **"Inner Work," "He," "She," "We," "The Fisher King and the Handless Maiden," "Ecstasy," "Transformation,"** and many others.

Bob Johnson is a well-respected Jungian psychoanalyst and a gifted, prolific writer. All of his books are surprisingly brief but carry very powerful, insightful messages. He uses mythological stories to help make his points. One book of his I recommend for everyone is **"Inner Work."** I've read a lot of books on how to understand the valuable messages available from our dreams but this one book does a great job of taking what can be a very dry subject and brings it to life.

David R. Hawkins MD, PhD **"Power vs Force"**

As a physician, I've literally read thousands of books both for professional and personal reasons. Some of what I've read has stayed with me to enrich my life. Unfortunately, I've also read much that I now wish I could get the time back. Over the years, I've been drawn to certain authors and every once in a while, found an author whose writings were so compelling that I experienced them as life-changing. Such it has been with the writings and lectures of Dr. Hawkins.

I count the day someone recommended I read Dr. Hawkins' first book, **"Power vs Force,"** as a seminal moment in this lifetime. To say it changed my experience of life and the direction of my personal journey is an understatement. I had spent a lifetime searching for Truth and even though I had been exposed to great wisdom in many forms, I had always felt the need to find a true Teacher of Truth. When I found Dr. Hawkins,

I found that Teacher. And I'm not alone. There are those who affirm that Hawkins was (he died September 19, 2012) the most Realized human in many centuries. The assertion that he had attained full Enlightenment is hard to validate using linear measures but if his state of evolution is measured by the results of his Teachings, then he surely was fully Enlightened.

Dr. Hawkins' books are not easy to read, but I personally know of a man with less than a 6th grade education, who had never read a newspaper, yet was able to read, understand, and absorb the lessons in "**Power vs Force**." It took him a year but he got through it. He, like so many others, claim it greatly enriched his mind and inner sense of peace.

One can find a lot of short clips of Dr. Hawkins' lectures on YouTube. I strongly recommend that one read **"Power vs Force"** as well, because it contains insights that will make understanding his Teachings much easier. There is so much to be gained by making an intensive study of Dr. Hawkins' Teachings that I urge the reader to give him a try.

"Power vs Force" was the first book in a trilogy. It was followed by **"Eye of the I"** and "**I,**

Reality and Subjectivity." I can personally attest that what is contained in these three books has been of more value to me than the sum total of the thousands of books I've absorbed in this lifetime. If you want to find Truth and a very clear path to an ever expanding tranquil serenity, read and reread and reread these three books. I personally have reread **"Eye of the I"** at least 15 times and it sits on my night stand to be opened at random as the first thing I absorb after I've gotten off my knees in the morning, asking for another day of Grace.

SUMMARY

I have attempted to make a few key points about what is possible in recovery. I've tried to show that many program members are simply settling for contentment instead of a true freedom of the spirit. I've attempted to provide a broader context in which to understand the underlying reasons that most people in recovery never fully achieve the potential suggested in The Promises.

We have looked at the importance of the paradigms within which we view things and the reality that no problem can be solved within the paradigm that created the problem in the first place. We have seen that the only proven way to overcome an addiction is to move into the non-linear paradigm of unconditional Lovingness. We have talked about paradigm allegiance and paradigm blindness and how these ways of doing life trap us in the old ways of the past, and limit our recovery potential.

We have explored the metaphor of our journey in recovery as being similar to climbing a great mountain. I've offered some ways of measuring our progress in recovery within this metaphor. We have seen that our journey up the mountain becomes easier when we start to view that journey from a grander context that only comes with the courage of venturing outside the box of our old ways of thinking.

We have looked at a few of the tools that we might consider using to break free from the trapped old material that may be limiting our progress. In addition, I've recommended a few books and authors that can potentially help us take our recovery to the next level.

Most of all, it is hoped that everyone who has read this book now has a solid understanding of just how important reducing the power of the ego is in achieving serene recovery. That goal needs to take top priority right behind achieving and maintaining abstinence.

It is hoped that we have been able to make the point that the quality of what can be achieved in recovery has no limit. No matter how good we feel about where we are in our journey, there is always another level that can be achieved, that offers even greater freedom, peace of mind, and joy.

Are these extravagant promises? We think not. They can become progressively more richly experienced in our lives, sometimes quickly, sometimes slowly but will always materialize if we are willing to work for them.

God, grant us the serenity to accept the things we cannot change, the courage to change the things we can, and the wisdom to know the difference.

ADDENDUM

A quote from the Big Book, Alcoholics Anonymous

If we are painstaking about this phase of our development, we will be amazed before we are half way through. We are going to know a new freedom and a new happiness. We will not regret the past nor wish to shut the door on it. We will comprehend the word serenity and we will know peace. No matter how far down the scale we have gone, we will see how our experience can benefit others. That feeling of uselessness and self-pity will disappear. We will lose interest in selfish things and gain interest in our fellows. Self-seeking will slip away. Our whole attitude and outlook upon life will change. Fear of people and of economic insecurity will leave us.

We will intuitively know how to handle situations which used to baffle us. We will suddenly realize that God is doing for us what we could not do for ourselves.

Are these extravagant promises? We think not. They are being fulfilled among us – sometimes quickly, sometimes slowly. They will always materialize if we work for them.

This excerpt from Alcoholics Anonymous, pages 83-84, are reprinted with permission of Alcoholics Anonymous World Service, Inc ("AAWS")

ABOUT THE AUTHOR

Dr. George E. Griffin is a 1962 graduate of NYU College of Medicine. He is Board Certified in General Surgery and Addiction Medicine and for over 40 years has been actively involved with Addiction treatment in the US, Canada, Europe, and Asia.

Dr. Griffin is a retired, decorated senior officer of the US Navy Medical Corps. He served in Viet Nam and is a qualified Navy Deep Sea Diver, Submarine Medical Officer, and Radiation Health specialist. During his Navy career, Dr. Griffin Commanded hospitals and medical facilities in the US and Japan. He also served as a special assistant to two US Marine Corps Commandants as The Medical Officer, US Marine Corps.

Dr. Griffin lives in Keene, NH with his wife Susan, with whom he shares 7 children, 11 grandchildren, and 3 great grandchildren. Although over 80 he is still an avid weight lifter, yoga practitioner and continues to complete a marathon each year.